D0716440

ENVIRONMENTAL DISASTERS

ANN WEIL

R.I.C. Publications® Pty Ltd

Air disasters
Deadly storms
Earthquakes
Environmental disasters
Fires
Mountain disasters
Sea disasters
Space disasters
Terrorism
Volcanoes

First published SADDLEBACK PUBLISHING, INC.
Three Watson Irvine, CA 92618-2767

Published under licence 2005 by R.I.C. PUBLICATIONS® PTY LTD
PO Box 332 Greenwood 6924 Western Australia
www.ricgroup.com.au

Distributed by:
Australasia
R.I.C. Publications, PO Box 332, Greenwood 6924, Western Australia:
www.ricgroup.com.au
United Kingdom and Republic of Ireland
Prim-Ed Publishing, Bosheen, New Ross, Co. Wexford, Ireland:
www.prim-ed.com
Asia
R.I.C. Publications, 5th Floor, Gotanda Mikado Building,
2-5-8 Hiratsuka, Shinagawa-Ku Tokyo, Japan 142-0051:
www.ricpublications.com

Photo Credits: cover, page 26, Bettmann/Corbis; page 17, Nik Wheeler/
Corbis; page 37, Roger Ressmyer/Corbis; pages 39, 55, AFP/Corbis; page
47, Paul A. Souders/Corbis; page 48, Roy Corral/Corbis

ISBN 1 74126 321 2
Printed in Korea

CONTENTS

1	Introduction	4
2	London, 1952	10
3	Love Canal, 1970s	20
4	Hanford, 1943	30
5	*Exxon Valdez*, 1989	40
6	Chernobyl, 1986	50
7	Bhopal, 1984	56
Epilogue		62
Bibliography		63
Index		64

TIME LINE ▶▶▶▶

22 June 1969

> Cuyahoga River in Cleveland, Ohio, catches fire due to its chemical pollution.

22 April 1970

> The first Earth Day is celebrated. Earth Day is a yearly event that reminds us to take care of the environment.

Where is Cleveland?

CLEVELAND

KEY TERMS ▶▶▶▶

pollution
> something that harms the air, water or soil

ozone layer
> a part of the atmosphere that takes out some of the sun's harmful rays

acid rain
> rain that is harmful because it is mixed with polluted air

extinct
> no longer alive

Our planet is home to billions and billions of plants and animals. Living things need air and water to survive. They also need a place to live. This is their—and our—environment.

Pollution Threatens

Some disasters threaten our environment. Many are the result of pollution. Modern life produces a lot of wastes. We throw away plastic bags full of rubbish. A lot of this ends up in large dumps.

Water pollution kills fish and other animals. It can also make water unsafe to drink.

Fumes from cars pollute the air. Air pollution causes health problems for many people. It can also reduce the ozone layer high in the earth's atmosphere.

The ozone layer filters out some of the sun's harmful rays. Without this protection, more people may die of deadly skin cancers.

Air pollution also causes acid rain. Polluted air mixes with rain as it falls to the ground. Acid rain is a serious problem all over the world. It kills plants and animals.

Many species are becoming extinct because of acid rain. Acid rain also pollutes lakes. The fish in those lakes die. Acid rain can even wear away some old buildings.

We use wood to build homes and furniture. People also use wood to heat their homes. A lot of the world's paper supplies come from wood.

That's a lot of trees! But forests are disappearing. Many species of rainforest plants and animals are becoming extinct.

These problems could turn into environmental disasters. Some environmental disasters build up over long periods. Others can happen in an instant.

Industrial Accidents

Industries use chemicals to make things we use every day. Many of these chemicals are poisonous. Most industries are responsible and safe. But accidents do occur. Most industrial accidents are minor. Some are very serious. A few are environmental disasters.

What can we do? Recycle!

Recycling bottles, cans and paper is one way to reduce pollution. And it's something we can all do to help our environment. Recycling saves fuel. Using less fuel means less air pollution, too.

TIME LINE ▶▶▶▶

4 December 1952

> A thick, yellow smog covers London, England.

5 July 1956

> In response to the smog, the United Kingdom passes the *Clean Air Act.*

Where is London?

KEY TERMS ▶▶▶▶

industry

a business that uses machines
and often produces a lot of
pollution

smog

a mixture of smoke, chemicals
and fog

asthma

a condition that sometimes
makes it hard to breathe

London is the capital city of England. It is also a very old city. People lived in London hundreds of years ago.

At first, people heated their homes with wood. Later, they switched to coal. They burnt the coal in stoves. This made a lot of smoke.

In the 1800s, industries added to the air pollution. By the early 1900s, the air was very dirty. The people of London were used to the problem. They lived with smoky air for many years.

They didn't realise it was a killer waiting to strike.

What is Smog?

Smog is a mixture of smoke and fog. London is famous for its fog. The city is close to the sea. The air is moist. Fog is made up of tiny particles of water. It's like a cloud close to the ground.

London had fog long before the air became polluted. The fog had never been a problem before.

But smoke and fog can be a deadly combination. The air turns yellow-brown. It is hard to breathe. The smog can get so thick, it's even hard to see.

Smog can cause health problems. It can damage the lungs. It can cause some types of cancer. It can also make some illnesses much worse.

People with asthma are badly affected by smog. People with heart disease are more likely to suffer a heart attack.

Fifty years ago, people were not so aware of the dangers of smog. It took a disaster to force them to clean up their act.

The Great Smog

On 4 December 1952, a yellow cloud of smog covered London. It got worse and worse. Cars crawled through the streets. Drivers could see only a few metres ahead. Movies were cancelled. People could not see the screen.

Everyone noticed the smog was bad. But there were no warnings on the radio or television. At first, people did not realise this was an emergency.

Farm animals became sick and died. More people than usual were going to the hospitals. The smog was to blame.

The Great Smog lingered for five days. Finally it blew away. But not before it killed 4000 people.

Most died of lung and heart illnesses. Thousands more people died later from the effects of the smog.

The Great Smog forced London to address its air pollution problem. The government passed its first *Clean Air Act* in 1956.

People used cleaner fuels. Less smoke went into the air. London still has smog. But these changes have kept the Great Smog a thing of the past.

Los Angeles, 1970s

Los Angeles has a smog problem. It is one of the smoggiest cities in the United States.

Exhaust from millions of cars and trucks becomes trapped over the city by the Santa Monica and San Gabriel mountains. The smog was at its worst in the 1970s. Then laws were passed to reduce car fumes. This helped lower smog levels.

The Los Angeles smog

Meuse Valley, Belgium, 1930

There were many glass factories and other industries in the Meuse Valley. They produced a lot of smoke. In December, there was unusual weather. The pollution was trapped close to the ground.

The smoke mixed with a thick, misty fog. Within a few days, the smog made more than 600 people very sick.

People with heart problems and bad lungs were especially affected. But some young people also became seriously ill. About 60 people died.

Donora, Pennsylvania, 1948

America's first pollution tragedy occurred in the small town of Donora. There were many industries in Donora. These included an acid-making plant, a steel mill and a zinc production plant.

Pollution became trapped in the narrow valley. It mixed with fog. The smog affected almost half the population of Donora. About 6000 people became ill. Some had sore throats. Others had headaches. Their eyes burned. There were 20 deaths in three days.

TIME LINE ▶▶▶

1896

William Love begins digging a
canal near Niagara Falls, New
York.

1942

A chemical company starts
dumping toxic wastes into the
canal.

Where is Niagara Falls?

NIAGARA FALLS

DID YOU KNOW?

More than 400 different chemicals have been found in the Love Canal dump.

KEY TERMS

toxic
: very harmful

pesticides
: poisons used to kill animals, insects or plants

contaminated
: polluted or infected

In 1896, a man named William Love started digging a canal near Niagara Falls, New York. The canal was never completed. Instead, it became a huge dump. This place became known as Love Canal.

A Chemical Dumpsite

In the 1940s and early 1950s, a chemical company dumped about 20 000 tonnes of acids, pesticides and other toxic wastes into the canal. The dump was closed in 1953.

The chemical company covered the area with clay. This was supposed to seal the chemicals inside. It looked like empty land. But the chemical waste was just below the surface.

The chemicals were inside large metal drums. Some of the drums were old and rusted. Many damaged drums split open when they were dropped into the dump.

Over the years, the drums broke down. More and more drums leaked. The chemicals seeped into the ground. These chemicals were known to cause cancer. They also caused birth defects. Some of the acids were strong enough to burn through skin.

People Move in

The city of Niagara Falls grew. More and more people moved there. The city needed to build a new school. They decided to build it over the chemical dump.

They began building in 1957. This broke the clay seal. Some of the chemicals ended up on the surface. School children playing in the dirt got burnt. The chemicals irritated their skin.

New Homes are Built

By the 1970s, hundreds of families were living there. Most of them had no idea they were living on top of an environmental disaster.

Soon, many people who lived in the neighbourhood of Love Canal had health problems. There were mysterious illnesses.

People seemed sick for no reason. The rate of miscarriages and birth defects was much higher than average. People developed liver and kidney disease.

In 1977, the air around Love Canal smelt funny. It was the chemicals.

The chemicals were turning up everywhere. They were in backyards. They flowed through creeks. They were even in people's basements. These toxic wastes had travelled from the dump into people's homes.

Grass wouldn't grow on some lawns. People got sick after eating vegetables from their own gardens.

Enough is Enough!

It isn't easy to prove that a dump is causing health problems. But one Love Canal resident was determined to do just that.

Lois Gibbs studied the problem. She organised the community. At first, the government refused to help. Eventually, they were forced to accept the facts. The dump was poisoning the people of Love Canal.

People were told to leave their homes. It cost over $30 million to evacuate the area. The residents were given money to move.

The message on the sign refers to the toxic chemicals in the ground below the veranda of this home in Love Canal.

The Government Steps in

The government bought their houses. Many homes were torn down. Love Canal was declared a disaster area.

It took 20 years and $250 million to clean up Love Canal. The toxic waste is still buried there. There is a fence around the dump site.

The Love Canal disaster received a lot of attention. People all over America learnt of the dangers of toxic wastes. They also discovered there were many more 'Love Canals' all over the country.

Billions of dollars were spent cleaning up other contaminated areas. Some states passed laws to control how industries disposed of their wastes.

Now Love Canal has been tested. It has been declared a safe place to live. Love Canal is now called Black Creek Village.

Times Beach, Missouri, 1982

In 1982, the people of Times Beach made an awful discovery. A man named Russell Bliss had been paid to get rid of a load of dioxin.

Dioxin is a very poisonous chemical. Bliss mixed the dioxin with waste oil. Then he sprayed it on dirt roads in Times Beach. He said it would control the dust. But it ended up destroying the town.

Dioxin does not break down in water or soil. It ended up in the Meramec River. Then the river flooded. The floodwater spread dioxin over the town. Times Beach became unlivable. Everyone had to leave. Times Beach was once home to about 2000 people. Now it is a ghost town.

TIME LINE ▶▶▶

March 1943

> The first nuclear power plant is built in Hanford, Washington. The plant makes plutonium for atomic bombs.

6 August 1945

> The United States drops the first atomic bomb on Hiroshima, Japan.

Where is Hiroshima?

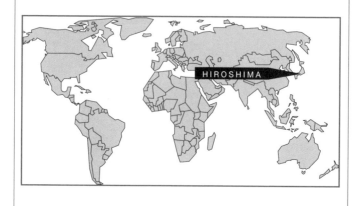

KEY TERMS ▶▶▶▶

atomic bomb

a weapon of mass destruction that causes a powerful, hot explosion

radioactive

giving off energy as a result of the breakdown of atoms

filter

a device that makes air or water clean

In 1943, the first nuclear plant was built in Hanford, Washington. This plant made radioactive plutonium. This was an essential ingredient for building the atomic bomb.

Plutonium from Hanford was in the atomic bomb that ended World War II.

Over the years, Hanford produced enough plutonium for many nuclear weapons. It also produced tonnes and tonnes of deadly nuclear waste. By the 1980s, Hanford was an environmental disaster.

World at War

Nuclear weapons were first used in World War II. Scientists had known the theory behind an atomic bomb before then. But no-one had made one. With the world at war, the pressure was on to build a better bomb.

In 1942, American scientists began working on a top secret project. It was called the Manhattan Project. They wanted to build the first nuclear weapon.

The stakes were very high. Other countries were also rushing to build an atomic bomb. It was a race to see who would make one first. And whoever won this race would win the war.

The A-bomb

The Americans won the race—and the Allies won the war. The atomic bomb (or A-bomb) was the first nuclear weapon. It's called a nuclear weapon, because its power comes from the nucleus of an atom.

There is a lot of energy locked inside the nucleus of each tiny atom. The A-bomb releases this energy as tremendous heat and a huge shockwave. Buildings and people are burnt to ashes. Deadly radiation contaminates the earth and water.

The A-bomb exploded atoms of plutonium. Each bomb needed only about 6 kilograms of plutonium. That's a piece of plutonium about the size of a cricket ball. It could produce an explosion capable of destroying an entire city.

Hanford: The Early Years

The Hanford nuclear plant was built in 1943. It produced most of the plutonium used in the first atomic bombs. It was the first plant of its kind. There were no safety standards for nuclear plants then. The scientists were focused on winning the war.

Radioactive materials were released into the air around Hanford. The first few years were the worst. But people did not know what was happening.

The government had said the plant was safe. But radiation is invisible. The amounts were never high enough to kill people immediately.

It wasn't until 1986 that the public learnt the truth. The government finally released the information.

Between 1944 and 1947, large amounts of radioactive materials escaped into the air. Much of this was in the form of radioactive iodine. It went up the smokestacks of the reactor.

This problem was eventually solved. Special filters were put inside the smokestacks. The filters trapped the radioactive iodine. It no longer escaped into the air. The public was no longer exposed to high levels of radiation.

But another problem was not so easy to solve. The plant operated for about 50 years. It produced a lot of nuclear waste. There were 2000 waste sites. Nearly half a million kilograms of radioactive uranium and plutonium were buried there.

About a quarter of a billion litres of deadly radioactive wastes were buried in underground tanks. Some of these tanks leaked. Contaminated liquids ended up in the soil.

It will take many years to clean up Hanford. The government is still working out how to tackle this huge environmental mess. Some estimate it will take 40 years. When it is completed, the final chapter on this historic nuclear plant will have ended.

Hanford's reactor was completed in 1944 and soon began making plutonium that was used in the first atomic bombs.

Plutonium in Outer Space

There is radioactive plutonium on the moon. Astronauts left it there. It provides power for instruments on the moon's surface. One kilogram of plutonium generates enough heat to run the system for 80 years.

Nuclear technology also powers space exploration. Unmanned spacecraft (called probes) bound for Mars and Jupiter are powered by plutonium.

This shows the Mars Polar Lander (MPL) spacecraft on the Martian surface, in the South Polar Region.

DATAFILE

TIME LINE ▶▶▶▶

24 March 1989

> *Exxon Valdez* spills 40 million litres of crude oil in Prince William Sound, Alaska.

25 January 1991

> There is an oil spill of 1.3 million tonnes in Sea Island, Kuwait.

Where is Prince William Sound?

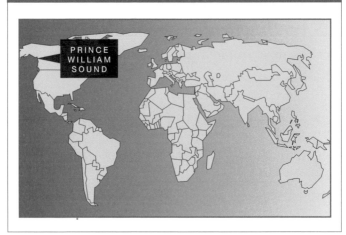

PRINCE WILLIAM SOUND

KEY TERMS ▶▶▶▶

tanker

a huge ship used to carry oil

reef

rock or coral that is near the water's surface

pipeline

a long line of tubes connected together

Chapter 5   *Exxon Valdez*, 1989

Most of us use some kind of fuel oil every day. It powers our cars. It heats our homes. Oil is transported on huge ships called tankers. Tankers travel the globe. A single tanker can carry millions of litres of oil. An accident can result in a disastrous oil spill.

That's what happened in Alaska in 1989. A tanker named the *Exxon Valdez* had just filled up with oil. It was on its way out of the port. The tanker was heading for California. But it didn't get very far.

Disaster Strikes

The accident happened just after midnight on 24 March 1989. The captain was asleep. The person steering the tanker was not experienced. There was floating ice in the bay. The crew changed course to avoid hitting it. But then they didn't correct their course.

The *Exxon Valdez* struck a reef. The rocks punched a hole in the ship. Forty million litres of oil flowed out into Prince William Sound.

Wildlife Hit Hard

Waves and tides spread the oil. Some of the oil reached the shore. It ended up covering over 2000 kilometres of the Alaskan coast.

The thick, black oil formed a sticky film over the beaches. Birds were the hardest hit. The total number of bird deaths will never be known.

One estimate is as many as 250 000. Entire bird colonies were wiped out.

Thousands of rare sea otters were killed. Seals and killer whales also died from the oil.

Some animal populations bounced back, years later. There are as many bald eagles now as there were before the spill. But others never recovered.

Pink salmon was one of Alaska's best-selling fish. But salmon fishing was stopped after the spill. No-one would buy salmon from polluted water.

For years, salmon eggs did not hatch properly. The oil spill was to blame. But this problem did not last forever. Over the years, the number of salmon increased. Salmon fishing started again.

Clean-up

Millions watched this drama on television. Pictures of birds covered in black crude oil were broadcast around the world. Many people volunteered to help.

But the clean-up was delayed. There were arguments over who would pay for it. The clean-up took three years. It cost more than $2 billion.

The ocean helped clean itself, too. Waves flushed out the oil. Sunlight and oxygen broke it down. But no clean-up is perfect. Prince William Sound is forever changed.

The *Exxon Valdez* was given a new name. It is now called the *SeaRiver Mediterranean*. It is still carrying oil around the world—but not to or from Alaska. The tanker is not allowed to enter Alaskan waters ever again.

Alaska Pipeline

The Alaska pipeline (Trans-Alaska pipeline) goes from Prudhoe Bay to Valdez. Prudhoe Bay is the largest oilfield in North America. Tankers can't go to Prudhoe Bay. It's too far north. There's too much ice in the water.

That's where the Alaska pipeline comes in. The oil is moved south along the Alaska pipeline. It ends up at Valdez. There, the oil is pumped onto tankers.

The pipeline is almost 1300 kilometres long. The pipe itself has a diameter of 1.2 metres.

'The Trans-Alaska pipeline'.

A volunteer tends to a sea otter injured in the Exxon Valdez *oil spill at the sea otter rescue centre in Valdez, Alaska. The tanker ran aground on Bligh Reef in Alaska's Prince William Sound on 24 March 1989, spilling 40 million litres of crude oil.*

TIME LINE ▶▶▶

28 March 1979

Radioactive gas escapes at Three Mile Island nuclear plant in Pennsylvania.

26 April 1986

A nuclear reactor catches fire and burns for two weeks in Chernobyl, a city in the Soviet Union.

Where is Chernobyl?

CHERNOBYL

Nuclear reactors split atoms of uranium. This generates a lot of heat. The heat is used to convert water to steam. The force of the steam turns a machine that generates electricity.

KEY TERMS ▶▶▶▶

nuclear reactor

a device that produces nuclear energy

generate

to make

radiation

a form of energy that can cause cancer and other health problems

fallout

the radioactive particles that fall after a nuclear explosion

There are nuclear power plants in many countries. They use nuclear energy to generate electricity. This electricity powers homes and businesses. People all over the world rely on nuclear power.

Most nuclear power plants operate safely. But an accident at a nuclear power plant can mean disaster.

Fire!

In April 1986, there was an explosion at a nuclear power plant in the Soviet Union. The nuclear reactor caught fire. The reactor burnt for two weeks.

Firefighters risked their lives to put out the blaze. Tonnes of radioactive materials were blown into the air. The Russian government reported that 31 people died. Thousands more were exposed to high levels of radiation.

High doses of radiation may not kill someone immediately. But they can cause cancer and other health problems years later. More than 100 000 people who lived near the nuclear power plant were told to leave their homes. But the threat was not limited to Chernobyl.

Russian cities kilometres away were also affected. Radioactive dust fell on towns and cities long distances from the accident. Some cities hosed down the streets with water. They tried to rinse the dust away.

The nuclear fallout went beyond Russia. Radioactive ash and dust had formed a deadly cloud. Wind and rain pushed the cloud over Europe. It spread over 1600 kilometres.

Sweden was the first European country affected. Farms there were ruined. The vegetables and soil were no longer usable. Even years after the accident, the ground was contaminated. Sheep in Scotland were also contaminated. So were reindeer in Finland.

What Caused the Explosion?

Workers at the Chernobyl nuclear power plant caused the accident. They turned off part of the machinery. The reactor heated up. Rods inside the reactor melted.

Uranium leaked into the water used for cooling the reactor. The water got boiling hot. Steam built up inside the reactor. The pressure of the steam blew up the top of the reactor.

It went through the roof of the power plant. There was a second explosion when cool air from outside came in contact with the red-hot core of the reactor.

Clean-up

Trees around the nuclear power plant were cut down. They were not burnt. That might have made radioactive smoke. Everything was buried under concrete.

An engineer at the Chernobyl power plant turns off the last reactor, closing the plant that caused the world's worst nuclear accident.

TIME LINE ▶▶▶▶

3 December 1984

Deadly gas leaks out of a pesticide factory in Bhopal, India.

3 December 1999

Environmental and human rights groups observe the first 'No Pesticide Day'.

Where is Bhopal?

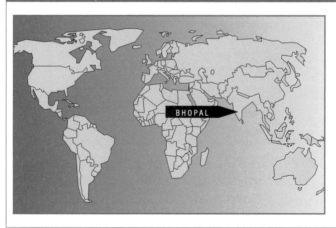

DID YOU KNOW? ▶▶▶

Air currents carry pesticides long distances. In the cold Arctic region, the gas turns to a solid. It ends up in the ice and snow. High levels of poisonous chemicals have been found in polar bears, seals and people too.

KEY TERMS ▶▶▶

clinic

a place where doctors examine and treat patients

Union Carbide

a large company that owned the Bhopal pesticide factory

Some farmers use pesticides to kill insects that eat their crops. Chemical pesticides contain strong poisons. They are made in factories. An accident at a pesticide factory can be a disaster.

Poisonous Gas Escapes

In 1984, poisonous gas escaped from a pesticide factory in India. It was one of the worst industrial accidents ever.

A deadly cloud of gas swept over the city of Bhopal. Thousands of people were killed. Some died immediately after breathing the gas.

More than 8000 died within 48 hours. Thousands more died later from the effects of the poison. The gas blinded some people instantly. Others had serious eye injuries.

The poison caused many health problems in the survivors. It damaged their lungs and other organs. This disaster seriously affected more than 80 000 people. And these awful effects are still with many of them today.

Fifteen Years Later

Even 15 years after the accident, survivors were still struggling. A clinic in Bhopal reported that 10 to 15 Bhopal survivors died each month. They also reported that 40 to 80 gas victims came to them every day for medical help.

The Bhopal pesticide factory was owned by Union Carbide. Union Carbide is a very large company. Some people blamed Union Carbide for the accident.

But the company claimed the accident was not their fault. They said an angry worker caused the accident on purpose.

Still, Union Carbide paid $470 million to the Indian government in 1989. Each victim was to receive about $500.

Some Indians feel this was not enough. Most of the victims were very poor. After the accident, they were too sick to work. They didn't have money to pay for medical help.

Doctors Still Seek Answers

Some doctors in Bhopal are still trying to find out more about the poison gas. They want to know which chemicals it contained. This may help them treat their patients better. They accused Union Carbide of keeping this information secret.

The fifteenth anniversary of the accident was on 3 December 1999. Human rights and environmental organisations then made it a special day for action. They're working to make sure there are no more Bhopal disasters.

Epilogue

Our health depends on the health of our environment. The US Environmental Protection Agency (EPA) was created in 1970. The EPA has a mission to protect human health. They work to make the land, air and water safe in the United States of America.

Every year, the EPA gives out President's Environmental Youth Awards. Young people who do projects to help the environment may win this award.

In 2002, a team of high school students in Skykomish, Washington won an award. They made two videos about a problem in their community. There was oil leaking from an old railroad fuelling station. These students inspired people to fix the problem.

Bibliography

Alcraft, Rob. *Oil disasters*. World's Worst. Des Plaines, IL: Heinemann Library, 2000.

Brennan, Kristine. *The Chernobyl nuclear disaster*. Great Disasters, Reforms and Ramifications. Philadelphia: Chelsea House, 2002.

Dils, Tracey E. *The* Exxon Valdez. Great Disasters, Reforms and Ramifications. Philadelphia: Chelsea House, 2001.

Riddle, John. *Bhopal*. Great Disasters, Reforms and Ramifications. Philadelphia: Chelsea House, 2002.

Sherrow, Victoria. *Love Canal: Toxic waste tragedy*. American Disasters. Berkeley Heights, NJ: Enslow Publishers, 2001.

Index

acid rain, 7

atomic bomb, 32-35

Bhopal, 58-61

cancer, 7, 13, 23, 53

Chernobyl, 52-55

Clean Air Act, 15

Exxon Valdez, 42-45

Gibbs, Lois, 25

Hanford, 32-37

London, 12-15

Love Canal, 22-27

Niagara Falls, 22, 23

nuclear waste, 32, 36

oil, 42-45

pesticides, 22, 58, 60

pollution, 6, 7, 12, 15, 18, 19

Prince William Sound, 43, 45

radiation, 34-36, 53

smog, 13-15

Union Carbide, 60, 61